UNTIL SOMEONE LISTENS

LISTENS

A Story About **BORDERS, FAMILY,**
and One Girl's **MISSION**

ESTELA JUAREZ
with **LISSETTE NORMAN**

illustrated by
TERESA MARTÍNEZ

Roaring Brook Press
New York

My family used to live together, in a house full of love. The yummy smell of my mom's flautas would bring us all to the kitchen.

The palm trees outside leaned toward our home
like they wanted to come inside and belong.

My mom said I got my energy and curiosity from her.
My older sister, Pamela, was more like my dad—
calm and quiet as a sunset.

I could count the words my dad said in a day on two hands,
but his words were always warm, just like my sister's hugs.

I had to go everywhere my mom went
because I moved fast like a colibrí,
a hummingbird.

As soon as I woke up, I would take off,
on a quest for answers.
I knew I would find what I needed because, just like my mom,
I carried hope in my wings.

My mother carried hope in her
when she left Mexico, where she was born,

to come to the other side of the river
in search of a better future.

Even though she was young and alone in a new country,
my mom was brave and determined to make a new life.

She went to high school.

She worked as a nanny

and a waitress.

She dreamed of becoming a lawyer one day.

My mom fell in love with someone who fought
for the country she was now a part of.
He was a United States marine.
A year after they married, my sister arrived.
I was born eight years later.
Like a curious little colibrí, I would go, go, go.
And sometimes as a family, we would fly together.

When I was four, a man from the government came to our house.
He said my mom had to go back—
to the other side of the river—
because she wasn't born in this country.

From then on, I never left her side.
I was scared to know a world without her in it.

Who would be there to kiss me before I went to sleep?

My mom and dad asked the government
again and again to let her stay.
She did everything they told her to do,
but nothing changed.

Even though no one would listen to them,
my parents kept trying.

Years passed. A new president came,
and it got worse.
No one could give us an answer.

My mom began having nightmares about leaving us.
She ran through the streets of our neighborhood,
trying to think of other ways to stay.

Then one August morning, that nightmare became real.
It felt like someone ripped us in half.

My mom didn't do anything wrong. She was just born somewhere else.
Some see people like my mom as ugly weeds that need to be plucked
out of the dirt. But they're not weeds.
They're wildflowers, all with pretty shapes and colors,
each one a different kind of beauty.

Waking up in a house without my mom that first day
was the hardest of all.

My sister gave me extra hugs and kisses at night.

My dad promised, "We'll all be together soon."

But soon wouldn't come soon enough.
Until then, I was a cloud—a gloomy cloud that sits and stays.

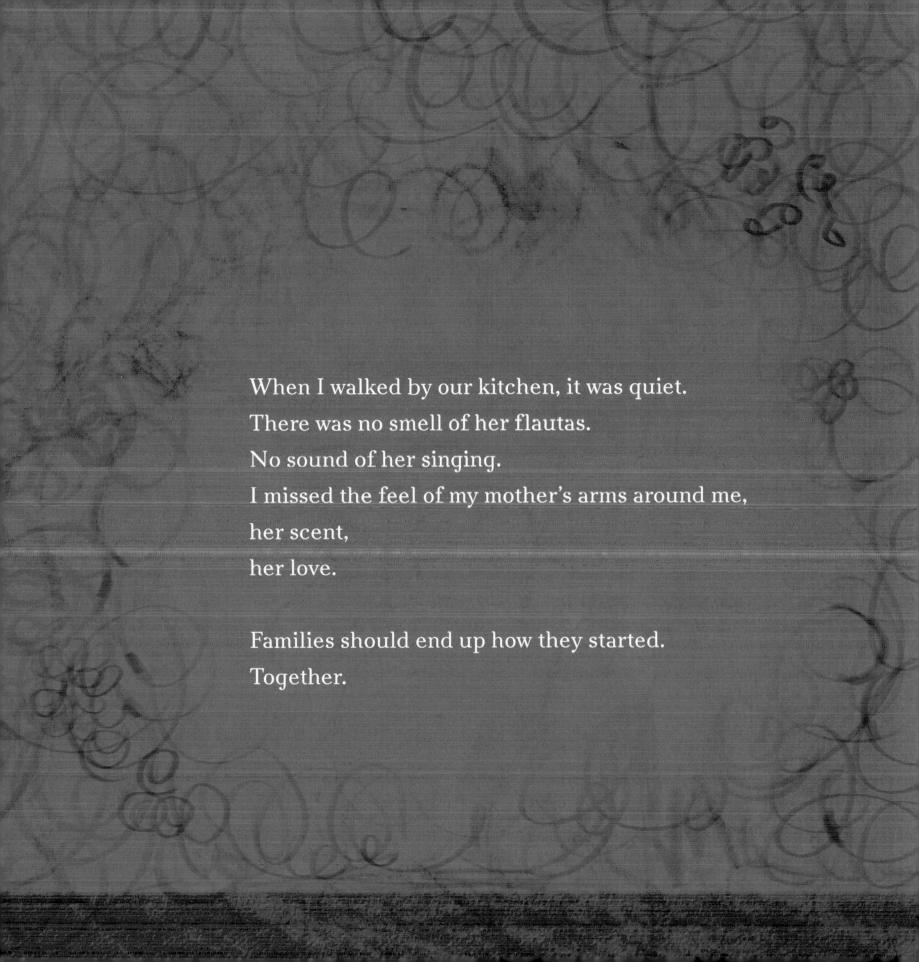

When I walked by our kitchen, it was quiet.
There was no smell of her flautas.
No sound of her singing.
I missed the feel of my mother's arms around me,
her scent,
her love.

Families should end up how they started.
Together.

We were one family

in two countries

but still together in our hearts.

At home, my dad and Pamela made me strong enough to fly far.

Since my mom couldn't come home,
my parents decided I would go live with her for a while.

Even though my heart broke a second time
when I said goodbye to my dad and sister,
I was excited to see my mom again.
But I shouldn't have had to leave my own country just to see her.
It wasn't fair.

I knew I had to do something.

At first, I read.
Then I wrote.

And wrote.

It was all I could think to do.
I turned what I wrote in my diary
into a letter to Congress.
I wrote a letter to the president.

I wrote letters to newspapers, to anyone who could help.
Anyone who would listen.

When I had to leave my mom again, my quest for answers
became more important than ever.

I discovered my words have power.
My voice has power too.
And I won't stop using my voice
until someone listens . . .

until my family is together again.

Every time I see a hummingbird, I feel my mom near.
I imagine her running through the streets of Yucatán,
wishing she were a colibrí,

flying back to me,

flying back to *us*.

AUTHOR'S NOTE

MY FAMILY, LIKE SO MANY OTHERS, was separated by unfair immigration laws.

My mom came to the United States in 1998, at the age of eighteen, in search of a better life. For the next fifteen years, she and my father worked to build their American dream in Florida. They started their own business and bought a house, where I grew up with my sister and our dog, Spot.

In 2013, an immigration officer knocked on our door. He told my mom she had to go back to Mexico, where she was born, because she was "undocumented." I was four years old. My mom explained to me and my sister that "undocumented" is what you call a person who doesn't have the papers that allow people from one country to live in another country. I called them *miracle papers*. The officer said my mom had to report to the immigration office the next day.

President Barack Obama's administration gave my mom permission to stay in the United States as long as she obeyed the laws and checked in with the immigration office every two years.

But when the next president was elected, he changed the immigration laws. During a routine visit, an immigration officer told my mom she had to go back to Mexico—and she had to report to their office every week until her deportation date.

The new president did not care that my dad fought for this country as a United States marine or that my mom was a military wife. No matter how many times my parents asked the government if she could stay, she was told she had to leave.

My mom couldn't apply to be a US citizen because, when she entered this country, she signed a paper at the border. She didn't understand any English or that the paper said she was breaking a federal law. When a person signs that paper, they're forced to leave the country. Some may have to wait up to ten years before they can apply for a legal way to enter the United States. But other people, like my mom, are told they can *never* enter this country again.

My parents spoke to different lawyers and went to many court hearings. They also asked lawmakers in our state for help. No one could stop her deportation.

Estela's mom and dad—Alejandra and Temo—with Estela and her big sister, Pamela, during a trip to visit Alejandra in Mexico.

On August 3, 2018, my mom was forced to return to Mexico. Heartbroken, I knew I had to do something. I was eight years old when I decided to write a letter to President Donald Trump about how his administration *separated* my military family, instead of protecting it. The video of my message to the president was played on major television news channels. And because of all the media attention, I was invited to do another video reading a letter to President Trump, to be shown at the 2020 Democratic National Convention, where Joe Biden

Estela, Alejandra, and Pamela in front of the Capitol Building in Washington, D.C.

was running for president. Congressman Darren Soto of Florida officially honored my sister and me as "Distinguished Daughters of Florida." Lawyers heard my message and offered to help reunite my family.

I soon discovered that there was power in my words and in my voice. I vowed to use my voice until my mom was back with us.

I went to live with her in Mexico for a year and a half so she wouldn't be alone, but I returned to Florida to be with my dad and sister after the Covid-19 pandemic began. Being separated from her was very painful for all of us. Our hearts broke every time she missed birthdays, holidays, special days like my sister's high school graduation, and difficult moments like the passing of our dog, Spot.

I would often dream of the day my mom came home. Inspired by John Lewis's book *March*, I wrote this book to continue to share our story. And I didn't stop until someone finally listened—and my dream of her return became real. On May 8, 2021, my mom was allowed to temporarily reunite with us in the United States. We are so grateful to the new president, Joe Biden, for making this possible. Now, as my parents try to figure out a way for my mom to stay permanently, we are working to heal our family.

RESOURCES FOR KIDS WHO WANT TO LEARN MORE

My Name Is Not Refugee by Kate Milner

Where Are You From? by Yamile Saied Méndez

Mama's Nightingale: A Story of Immigration and Separation by Edwidge Danticat

La Frontera: El viaje con papá / My Journey with Papa by Deborah Mills and Alfredo Alva (bilingual)

Estela's DNC video, youtube.com/watch?v=cevWk5MSeHo

For my mother, Alejandra Juarez—the strongest woman I know—who taught me
to be strong and kind, and to follow my dreams.

And for Pentagon correspondent Tara Copp, who first reported about my mother
and kept her story alive, even after she left the United States.

Publishing my first book was possible due to the help of a team of wonderful people: Thanks so much to my editor,
Connie Hsu, for believing in the story of my family. It has been a dream to work with you. Thanks to the amazing
team at Macmillan Publishers for supporting and bringing this book to as many kids as possible. Thanks to the
wonderful Teresa Martínez—your illustrations are glorious. Thanks to Lissette Norman: You are the best writing
partner. We should do it again! Finally, thanks to my wonderful literary agent, Johanna V. Castillo, for dreaming
with me and helping me become a published author. Special thanks to the organizations that helped reunite my
family—FWD.us and Resilience Communications—and the many, many people who offered their time and support.

—E. J.

To Mom, Ma Teresa, with love

—T. M.

Published by Roaring Brook Press
Roaring Brook Press is a division of Holtzbrinck Publishing Holdings Limited Partnership
120 Broadway, New York, NY 10271 · mackids.com

Text copyright © 2022 by Estela Juarez
Illustrations copyright © 2022 by Teresa Martínez

Library of Congress Cataloging-in-Publication Data is available.
ISBN 978-1-250-83212-2

Our books may be purchased in bulk for promotional, educational, or business use.
Please contact your local bookseller or the Macmillan Corporate and Premium Sales Department at
(800) 221-7945 ext. 5442 or by email at MacmillanSpecialMarkets@macmillan.com.

First edition, 2022
Printed in China by RR Donnelley Asia Printing Solutions Ltd., Dongguan City, Guangdong Province
1 3 5 7 9 10 8 6 4 2

The illustrations in this book were created digitally, and the text was set in Bachenas.
The book was edited by Connie Hsu, designed by Cindy de la Cruz, and art directed by Sharismar Rodriguez and Neil Swaab.
The production editor was Jennifer Healey, and the production was managed by Susan Doran.